# The Meaning of Christmas

## James Philip

This revised edition first published by Tron Books, 2024,
© William J U Philip 2024

Cover design: Megan Hogarth
Cover artwork: Rizwan Saqib

Previously published by Holyrood Abbey Church:
First Edition 1971
Enlarged Edition 1977
Reprinted 1982



Paperback ISBN: 978-1-917493-01-7
ePub ISBN: 978-1-917493-02-4

# Contents

# Preface

This book is a series of meditations on the real message, and meaning, of Christmas. Taking some of the most familiar words from the Bible commonly associated with the Christmas season, they seek to unpack not just the familiar story of the nativity, but its true and abiding significance for our world.

Originally, they formed the substance of Christmas sermons given by my father, James Philip, in Holyrood Abbey Church, Edinburgh, mostly during the 1960s – though one might be forgiven for thinking they could have been written today, such are the striking contemporary parallels in places to life some six decades on. (The Scripture quotations, however, bear testimony to that time; we have retained, mostly, the Authorised Version as originally used. Often, in fact, it is these words from the AV which are most familiar to many from Christmas readings in traditional Lessons and Carols services.)

My father, a fine musician, loved playing the music of Christmas, and singing the carols of Christmas; he also loved the excitement of Christmas, the celebration and drama of

Christmas services, and the atmosphere of joy that pervades them. But above all, he loved preaching at Christmas. He loved to preach on the Incarnation because the sheer wonder of it never ceased to thrill his heart all over again as he immersed his mind afresh, year by year, in the unfathomable mystery of *God* manifest in the *flesh*. That the One through whom 'all things were made', as the Nicene Creed declares, 'for us men and for our salvation...came down from heaven, and by the Holy Spirit was incarnate of the Virgin Mary, and became man' was, to him, the greatest message which could ever be told, or heard.

His was a mind which drank deeply at the wells of biblical truth, and he was able to synthesise and impart that truth in words bringing both light to the mind and delight to the heart. First published in 1971 (and several times thereafter) but long since out of print, my hope in producing this revised edition is that many more will find both light and delight in the *meaning* of Christmas.

**William J U Philip, 2024**

# I

# The Wonderful Name

*For unto us a child is born,*
*unto us a son is given:*
*and the government shall be upon his shoulder;*
*and his name shall be called*
*Wonderful, Counsellor,*
*the Mighty God,*
*the Everlasting Father,*
*the Prince of peace.*

(Isaiah 9:6)

The warm glow we feel at Christmas stems from something more than conventional sentiment; it is born of the very reality of the message of Christmas itself – Immanuel, God with us.

When the wise men from the east asked, 'where is he that is born king of the Jews?' they were probably not aware of how truly they spoke, or of the fact that their convictions echoed words spoken in ancient time by the prophet Isaiah who said, in words sublime and glorious, 'unto us a Child is born... and the government shall be upon his shoulder'. (What music there is in these wonderful words! George Frideric Handel certainly captured the sense of majesty that they contain in the immortal chorus from the *Messiah*; it is musical writing in the grand manner, worthy of the sublime theme it deals with.)

## Hope for a world in crisis

Allow me to sketch briefly the background against which these words were first spoken, to show their relevance for today. The picture in the closing verses of Isaiah 8 is a very dark one. It depicts the crisis that came on the northern kingdom, Israel,[1] in 732 B.C. when facing looming destruction by the Assyrian Empire. The storm clouds came on, and the people panicked and went to pieces, reverting to spiritism for help, cursing king and God as they went into darkness. But it was in the context of this atmosphere of national crisis that the vision was given to Isaiah of the coming Messiah, the King who would reign in righteousness, on whose shoulders the government was to rest.

The parallel with our own time is very striking and apt. In those days there was moral declension leading to anarchy and the breaking up of the fibre of the nation; in ours, we see growing violence, lawlessness and the need for nothing so much as a strong, stable hand on the reins of this world. It is in this context that the promise given by Isaiah gleamed with holy light and hope for the people of God in olden time; and it is thus also that we find hope in its fulfilment in the coming of Christ.

But even in the context of his having come, at last, the birth of Christ does not yet seem to have fulfilled the hopes either

1   After Solomon's reign, the kingdom was thereafter divided into two: Israel, comprising the 10 tribes to the north, and Judah, in the south, comprising Judah and Benjamin (See 1 Kings 12ff).

of Isaiah or of those who 'waited for the consolation of Israel' (Luke 2:25). Peace on earth, good will towards men – does it not all sound rather hollow in the face of all the convulsions and violence of the world's scene?

There are two things to be said about this. One is that the government really *is* upon his shoulder, but his kingship is a *hidden* one for the moment; the other is the deepest truth, that the best part of Christmas has not happened *yet*. We still live, in a very real sense, also like those of old who waited for the consolation of Israel. Let me say something about these two thoughts, the hidden King, and the King manifested.

## The present hiddenness – of this world's true King

There are two ways of looking at this idea of the hiddenness of the King.

One is to say that whereas now the King offers peace to those who believe on him, then – at his coming in glory – he will enforce it, as it is his right to do so. In this sense, his kingdom and his kingship remains hidden.

> How silently, how silently,
> the wondrous gift is given;
> so God imparts to human hearts
> the blessings of his heaven.
> No ear may hear his coming;
> but in this world of sin,
> where meek souls will receive him, still
> the dear Christ enters in.

## Sovereign authority revealed

The other way is to recognize that his coming at Bethlehem *did* in fact make a decisive change in the history of the world, a change which can be described in terms of an assumption of authority in the world.

The coming of the wise men from the east is a symbol of exactly this; it was the first assembly of the court come to do obeisance and homage to the King. And this fact is symbolic of the King's real authority and influence over men. They were drawn to his presence, and they were the first fruits of an innumerable multitude that have been drawn since, down the ages, by his power. This is not a romantic notion, but a sober fact. When the aged Simeon took the infant Redeemer in his arms in the Temple, he said, 'This child is set for the fall and rising again of many in Israel'. How truly he spoke, and to be this, you need power and authority to pull down and raise up. Exactly. The government of men was to be upon *his* shoulder.

Consider the story in Matthew Chapter 2. It is clear that the effect of his coming, even as a babe, was revolutionary in Jerusalem. The whole city, from the king down, was troubled – and this before he could say anything; simply being there was enough to create this effect.

Look at the whole record of the Gospels: Jesus was a penniless, wandering preacher, with nowhere to lay his head; but the wind and waves obeyed his will, sickness and disease took orders from him, demons owned his authority, and when he said to men, 'Follow Me' they forsook all and followed, recognising the royal command.

Viewed from one point of view – the purely human standpoint – one could describe his story as 'the failure of a mission'. He was crucified in weakness, and all his disciples forsook him and fled. Yet the record makes it plain that it was he, not his enemies, who called the tune. 'That thou doest, do quickly' he said to Judas (John 13:27), choosing his own time to die. Indeed, dying was the way he chose to establish and vindicate his kingship. 'I, if I be lifted up from the earth, will draw all men unto me' (John 12:32). This was his promise. And this is what was fulfilled. Look at the dying thief, the centurion, Joseph of Arimathea, Nicodemus. Read the Acts of the Apostles – the preaching of the cross became the power of God, and a whole world was turned upside down into a kingdom for Christ. Nothing that the desperate powers of darkness could do could overthrow his easy sovereignty. This is what the writers of the New Testament seek to convey, and this is the point of their writing. It is as if on every page they are saying, 'Look at the kingship of Christ; he is born a King, and he dies a King'.

Pilate was truer than he knew when he said to the Jews, 'Behold your King'. One can easily imagine the contempt and derision with which the Roman soldiers looked at this crucified figure. A King, forsooth! They were used to the great triumphal procession through Rome of their great emperors and military leaders. A King? Ah, yes, they just did not know. King Jesus has the government upon his shoulder, and has assumed his reign. The Roman Empire is no more.

The hidden King – yet perhaps not so hidden!

# The coming manifestation – of this world's true King

But now our second consideration: the manifestation of the King. The control he has, even now, over history, will one day be manifested openly.

It is sometimes hard for Christian people to believe that God in Christ controls history even now, but this is the unanimous testimony of the Scriptures, which make it very plain that evil has lost the initiative since Jesus Christ was born and lived and died and rose again. Evil does not now have the last word in the affairs of men. The government *is* upon his shoulder, but that hidden authority will be displayed openly to all only when Jesus comes to reign.

The real subject matter of the Christmas story, as indeed of the gospel, is neither the Babe of Bethlehem, nor the Man of Calvary, but Christ the Lord of glory. 'And our eyes at last *shall* see him'. This is the immeasurable hopefulness of the situation, however dark or anarchical things may be in the world of men. Scripture teaches us that the dark crises are but the birth-pangs of the new creation, and that out of them Christ will bring forth his victory and his peace.

This, whether we realise it or not, is the real joy of Christmas. The cradle points, through the cross, to the crown. Christ will come again, and every eye shall see him. And every knee shall bow, and every tongue confess that he is Lord, to the glory of God the Father.

## The blessing of his present rule

In the meantime, while the nations of men hold out in bitter opposition against his rule, the hearts of men and women may yield to his kingship and authority. He conquers there; and where he conquers, he blesses, and proves himself to be Wonderful, Counsellor, the Mighty God, the Everlasting Father, the Prince of Peace.

This is why we may take Isaiah's words to our hearts today. His name shall be called *Wonderful* – and when we get a real sight of our blessed Saviour, that is just what we feel; we think it is wonderful, for it fills all the need of our hearts, the emotional needs as well as the spiritual. *Counsellor* – are we walking in darkness, in perplexity? Here is a Counsellor to lead us and to guide our footsteps into the paths of peace. *The Mighty God* – do we have a sense of our weakness, our inability? Here is a God who is mighty, the El-Shaddai God. *The Everlasting Father* – what does this tell us? Just this, that in Christ we have come home to the Father's house, and we belong. They say Christmas is a family affair, and in the spiritual sense it most truly is. We have come home, and we are in the place where we belong and matter. *The Prince of Peace* – 'Come unto me', he says, 'and I will give you rest'. Peace is a princely gift, and it is ours in the gift of God's Son.

## The pledge of his permanent reign

For the Christian, Christmas is the time which reminds him of the great glad day for which the whole creation waits with eager longing. It is not only a foretaste, but a pledge of what one day will be, a harbinger of something that still lies in the future, just as the snowdrop is a harbinger of spring, telling us, as C.S. Lewis beautifully puts it, that we have turned the corner of the year. Summer is coming, but it is still some way off, and the snowdrops do not last long. But they prophesy, and even if further snowstorms come – as they often do – the signs of coming spring have been seen in their blooming.

We are still living in the frosts and cold east winds of the old order (and what a bitter winter it proves to be!). But the everlasting spring of God's love and grace is on the way, and Christmas is his gracious foretaste and reminder that we do not hope in vain.

**2**

# The Fullness of the Time

*When the fullness of the time was come,*
*God sent forth his Son, made of a woman,*
*made under the law, to redeem them that*
*were under the law, that we might receive*
*the adoption of sons.*

(Galatians 4:4-5)

The message of Christmas must be understood in *Christian* terms, that is to say, in the context of the gospel proclaimed by the Christian Church every other week throughout the year.

There is a deep theology in Christmas, and we must not miss it in the welter of celebrations of the festival. This tends to happen when the truth of the birth of Christ is separated from the rest of the gospel; the Bible, however, sees the event of Christ's coming as the epicentre of its entire message. In Paul's statement about the meaning of our Lord's coming in Galatians 4:4 the apostle says, 'When the fullness of the time was come, God sent forth his Son...'

What does he mean by the words 'When the fullness of the time was come'?

## God's plan of salvation

The language is suggestive. One might almost think that Paul was using military terms; he is certainly speaking of a divine strategy. Older divines used to speak of God's 'plan of salvation', and that was a true insight, for the testimony of the Scriptures is that there is such a plan, formulated in the councils of eternity, prepared for down the ages of Old Testament history, and brought to fruition in the fullness of the time, when Christ came to earth.

This is how the Scriptures invite us to view the gospel, and this is their central testimony: In the fulness of the time – at the strategic moment – something happened, something decisive, unique, once for all, the intervention of God, a visitation from on high, in which God has made himself known in grace and mercy to mankind. This is the principal affirmation of the Christian faith. To say anything less, or anything else, is to miss the mark completely. Christianity stands or falls on this basic reality; either this is true, or the whole fabric of the Faith falls to pieces. There can be no modification, for this is Christianity. James Denney has said, 'If God has really done something in Christ on which the salvation of the world depends, and if he has made it known, then it is a Christian duty to be intolerant of anything which ignores, denies or explains it away. The man who perverts it is the worst enemy of God and man'.

## The fullness of the time

Paul says that this divine intervention in history came 'in the fullness of the time', and this was so in a number of respects.

## Fulfilment of Israel's destiny

It was the fullness of the time firstly in relation to the Jewish people who were, so to speak, the repository of God's revelation. And this in two ways:

### *hope for the promised seed*

On the one hand, the whole Old Testament was a time of preparation for the coming of the promised Seed who was to bruise the head of the Serpent (Genesis 3:15). Abraham and his family were as clay in the hand of the potter, as with infinite patience and love God shaped and fashioned them into a people and a nation for his own possession, into an instrument of revelation to the world. For long centuries he bore with them, disciplining them, rebuking and chastising them in their stubbornness and self-will, until at the last there came a day when he visited them in grace, and the virgin Mary said, 'Behold the handmaid of the Lord: be it unto me according to thy word'.

### *humbling of the people's sin*

On the other hand, the advent of Jesus came as the culmination of ages of preparation in another sense, ages in which God patiently taught his people, by symbol and ordinance, by priest and prophet, not only the depth of the contradiction sin had wrought in the human heart, but also that no human means could ever resolve that contradiction.

It is this that explains the hope that becomes more and more evident down the ages of the Old Testament – the hope of a coming Messiah. This hope was consciously cherished, it is true, only by the spiritual remnant, but it is these who are represented at the beginning of the Christian era by such people as Zacharias and Elizabeth, Joseph and Mary, the shepherds, and Simeon and Anna who 'waited for the consolation of Israel'.

And the coming of Christ was when 'the fullness of time was come' and God's preparation in his people was complete. For his purpose and intention in the world, he had in that little group of people a lump of clay that was submissive in the Potter's hand, and this submission, this obedience, is summed up, as it were, in Mary's utterance, 'Behold the handmaid of the Lord, be it unto me according to thy word'. When God got his people to that point, it was the fullness of the time; the strategic moment had arrived.

## Fulfilment of the world's destiny

Furthermore, it was also the fullness of the time in relation to the secular world as a whole; God indeed chose his strategic moment perfectly for the coming of his Son. The ancient world had been opened up by Roman civilisation and Roman administration. Everywhere there were fine roads that Rome had built. Travel and communication were, comparatively speaking, easy. Furthermore, the other main means of communication – language – was utterly propitious to the spreading of the gospel. Greek was the then world language, and so the language barrier was, for the first Christian missionaries, non-existent.

The ancient world was ready in another sense too, for old mythological religions had sickened and disgusted intelligent people. It was a world full of despair and frustrated hopes, a lost world. One of its philosophers said, 'The best thing of all is not to be born, and the next best thing is to die'. That was the spirit that prevailed in the ancient world when Jesus came, and people's hearts were hungry – as may be seen from the words spoken in Paul's vision of the man from Macedonia: 'Come over and help us'.

It was an age of intellectual, moral and spiritual bankruptcy; and to this world, at the strategic moment, at the time when the need was greatest, the Saviour came.

## Fulfilment of individual destiny

But what is true in the historical sequence can be said to be just as true of an individual life. There is a 'fullness of the time' for men, when they are brought to an end of themselves, either by the work of the law convincing them of sin, or by other varied means, the frustrations of life (which come from God in his providence), its disciplines and disappointments. Thus also does God prepare the way for the Saviour's coming.

# The sending of God's Son

We must note what Paul goes on to say in the next part of the verse. Christ came, he tells us, 'made of a woman, made under the law, to redeem them that are under the law'. What is implied here?

## The Son of God was born *as* man

John Calvin puts it this way: 'Christ the Son of God, who was by right exempt from all subjection, became subject to the law. Why? In one word, that he might obtain freedom for us'. And he adds, 'A free man redeemed a slave by constituting himself a surety: by putting chains on himself he takes them off the other'. Christ puts himself under the law, i.e. he enters into our life, into our situation, as a man – The Man, moreover, who did not need to have been a man at all, unless he had chosen; one as C.S. Lewis so graphically put it, 'who served in our sad regiment as a volunteer'. This is so important for two reasons.

## The Spirit of the Son is born *in* man

The first is this: Christ has entered into our life, into human life, once for all. And since that is so, Paul must go on in Galatians 4:6 to say something else: 'Because ye are sons, God hath sent forth the Spirit of his Son into your hearts, crying, Abba, Father'. Not only has God sent his Son into the world of men; he sends his Spirit into the hearts of men. And this is what takes Christmas out of the past into the present, out of the romance of history into the grim, despairing world of our time, to bring hope to us, and joy and peace. It was a true insight that made Wesley sing,

> Born to raise the sons of earth,
> Born to give *them* second birth.

This is the real issue of the mystery of the Incarnation: not merely that Christ should be born into the world, but that he should be born in us; not merely that there should be a virgin birth in Bethlehem, but also a virgin birth of faith in our souls; not merely that Christmas should have happened long ago, but that it should happen today to men and women, boys and girls.

Notice the twofold 'sending' – his *Son* into the world, his *Spirit* into our hearts: his Son, as John Stott puts it in his commentary on Galatians, to secure our sonship in the family of God, and his Spirit to assure us of the reality and blessedness of that sonship; his Son to give us the status of sonship, and his Spirit to give us the experience of it.

How wonderful it is to realise that his Spirit, bringing the knowledge and experience of the reality of the meaning of the Incarnation, comes to our hearts *in* the gospel offer, in the preaching of the good news. Apart from this there can be no real joy in Christmas – a man remains desolately, wistfully, outside the glory. He looks in, with hungry, longing eyes, but he does not enter into its reality.

## The substitution of the Son is *for* man

The second reason why the coming of Christ into our life is important is this: he has come into the world, and into our hearts, as God's blessed and all-sufficient Substitute for what we call life, vitiated and adulterated as it is by sin. He is now to be our life, in place of the tragic self-centeredness and pervertedness which have been all men's undoing.

Paul has said earlier, in Galatians 2:20, 'I have been crucified with Christ'. The 'I' – the 'Ego' that has been inverted and perverted against God and has stood in revolt against him and so against its true destiny – that 'I' has been crucified, put out of the way, set on one side, and replaced by a new life, a new kind of life, a new principle. It is the life of One who has overcome the dark enemy who has plagued human life since the beginning and defeated him for ever more – and therefore, gloriously, wonderfully, the Christian can say with Paul, 'I live, yet no-longer I, but Christ lives in me'.

In the last analysis there are only two possibilities for life, not many. Either it is 'to me to live is – *self*', a twisted, broken, aimless, hopeless, despairing, disillusioned, meaningless life – and how much of this we see all around us today, as the apostles saw in theirs; or, it is 'to me to live is – *Christ*', a borrowed life, a life in the love of God, in the family of God, in the favour of God, in the presence of God.

This is the thrust of Christmas, its challenge and its incredible offer of hope.

## The new birth of God's Spirit

I would like to think that there will be some honest thinking in people's minds at Christmas time – as they sing the wonderful carols and celebrate the Saviour's birth – asking themselves why they sing these lovely words, and what it is all about. 'God sent his Son into the world' – yes, but two thousand years ago; what has that to do with me?'

If all we have is the memory of something that happened two thousand years ago, the answer must be, 'nothing'; it is but a pious story, no more. But if it means this: 'God sent his Spirit *into our hearts*', then it means that Christmas is 'repeated', wonderfully and widely, and that the birth of the Saviour into the world becomes the birth of the Saviour in our hearts.

That is why the wonderful words spoken by the angel Gabriel to Mary in Luke 1:35 are so beautiful as an illustration of this glorious reality: 'The Holy Ghost shall come upon thee, and the power of the Highest shall overshadow thee; therefore also that holy thing which shall be born of thee shall be called the Son of God'. This is also what Paul is speaking about here.

In the fullness of the time God sent forth his Son, yes, once for all, in the strategic moment of history something happened, and Christ came. But this other thing is *not* once for all; it has been happening ever since. God has sent forth the Spirit of his Son into our hearts. And what that means is that Christmas, with all its beauty and glory and hallowed associations, is something that can *happen to you*. A holy birth can take place in your heart, the virgin birth of faith. The Holy Ghost comes upon a man, the power of the Highest overshadows him, and that holy thing that is born in him is called the Son of God.

> O Holy Child of Bethlehem,
> descend to *us* we pray;
> cast out *our* sin, and enter in;
> be born in *us* today.
> We hear the Christmas angels
> the great glad tidings tell;
> O come to *us*, abide with *us*,
> *Our* Lord Immanuel.

# 3

# The Benedictus

*The dayspring from on high hath visited us*

(Luke 1:78)

We need to be reminded these days of how easy it is to lose sight of the real meaning and message of Christmas, in the midst of the greater than ever commercialisation of the festive season.

All too often the real point of Christmas is missed, and that it comes and goes without anything of its significance being grasped, even by a great many who do centre their Christmas celebrations in the religious and spiritual sphere. Who would not love these glorious carols, or join in singing them? It is safe to say that there will be tens of thousands of people throughout the land in church at Christmas who do not normally or often attend worship. They come as if drawn by some instinct to the spiritual heart of the festival, without perhaps knowing why.

And yet the meaning of Christmas is clear and plain for all who will thoughtfully read the Christmas story in the Scriptures. Any of the several aspects or sections of the narrative gives a sufficient indication of the divine message which the Christmas mystery is meant to convey. We turn here to the *Benedictus*, that song of Zacharias which, for all its lyrical beauty, contains a whole system of divinity within its brief compass. The wonderful words at its very heart, 'the dayspring from on high hath visited us', rightly understood, convey all the wonder and blessedness of the Christmas message.

## Divine visitation

We should notice, in the first place, how and in what terms each of the three sings whose songs are recorded in the opening chapters of Luke's Gospel – Mary's *Magnificat*, Simeon's *Nunc Dimittis* and Zacharias' *Benedictus* – speak of the birth of the Saviour. Each considers it in terms of a *visitation* from God:

> 1:49 'He that is mighty hath done to me great things'
>
> 2:30 'Mine eyes have seen Thy salvation'
>
> 1:68 'He hath visited and redeemed His people'

However, we see first of all that Zacharias's response to the divine visitation was one of rank unbelief brought a judgment upon him. He stumbled through unbelief, unable apparently to grasp that all things are possible with God.

This is not the only case of impoverishment coming because of a refusal to believe, and we may learn, in the midst of the beauty of the Christmas message, that God means his Word to be taken seriously on pain of censure and punishment. He expects to be believed and obeyed. It does not do to question his power to do what he says.

# God's promise fulfilled

It is interesting, in relation to this, to see that Zacharias's song, the Benedictus, has to do with this aspect of truth, the fulfilment of what God has said of old; and this serves to teach us that when God brings us under discipline he awakens in us a new appreciation of what we had hitherto been prone to neglect. It was forgetfulness of the testimony of the Scriptures in past time that was Zacharias's sin. But in the nine long months he spent under the chastening of God he was given time to think again, and when at last his lips were opened he was singing a very different tune. Sometimes we have to learn the hard way – our spiritual obtuseness makes this inevitable.

The characteristic theme, then, of the Benedictus is the fulfilment of God's word and promise in the mystery of the Incarnation. As we see from verse 68, God's visitation of his people has taken place (i) in accordance with the words spoken by his prophets, (ii) in accordance with the promises made to the fathers, (iii) in remembrance and fulfilment of his holy covenant, and (iv) in accordance with the oath sworn to Abraham.

Now it is the idea of God's *covenant* that must be stressed here, and it is this that puts the Christmas message in its true perspective and context. The Incarnation is a new beginning; all that is said here indicates that this is so. But it is a new beginning that was prophesied and foretold down the ages, and which fulfilled the covenant God made with his people. It is a true insight in the lovely service of *Nine Lessons and Carols* that it takes us right back to Genesis 3:15, for that, human-wise, is where the covenant began and was instituted. Such is the grace of God: hard upon the fall of man came the promise of light, the promise that a new day would dawn for the human race. This was the gracious covenant that God made, and renewed and ratified to each succeeding generation, and this the meaning of the divine visitation that we know as Christmas.

# God's presence returned

Let us think about the meaning of this word 'visitation'. To say that God has visited his people in the coming of Christ does not mean a passing or temporary visit, as we use the word. A royal visit by the Sovereign is over in a day or two; but here God has come, and he has come to stay.

That is the first point. He has come to be with us forever. In the Incarnation God has entered human life once for all, and the gulf between God and man has been bridged for good. Nothing will ever destroy that link again. That is why the Christmas message is such good news. Communications between heaven and earth have been restored!

But more. This word 'visited' has a particular meaning in the Bible. It literally means that God has 'turned his face upon' his people. What this means is that God, whose face had been turned away from mankind because of sin, has now once for all been turned *towards* men in love and pity, and that now his thoughts toward us are thoughts of peace and not of evil. The words recorded in Acts 7:34 of God's promise to his beleaguered people in Egypt are an appropriate expression of what happened at Bethlehem:

'I have seen, I have seen, the affliction of my people which is in Egypt, and I have heard their groaning, and am come down to deliver them.'

Christmas speaks, therefore, of a reconciled face that has been turned towards the children of men.

This is why it is impossible to speak of the Incarnation without also including the Atonement and Reconciliation made in the cross of Christ, for this is what completes the visitation and makes it a visitation from God. The one is meaningless without the other. The Psalmist's prayer, 'God be merciful to us and bless us; and cause his face to shine upon us' (Psalm 67:1) is in fact answered fully in the message of Christmas.

## A new dawn for mankind

Next, we must consider the beautiful description of this divine visitation. Zacharias calls it 'the dayspring from on high'. Thoughtful commentators have seen here a reference to the prophecy in Malachi 4:2, 'But unto you that fear my name shall the Sun of righteousness arise with healing in his wings'. And it is quite certain that what happened on that first Christmas is described in this ancient prophecy.

This is what gives the clue to the real meaning of Zacharias's words. The word 'dayspring' literally means 'sunrising', and the idea it is meant to express is that in the coming of the Saviour a *new day has dawned* for the world. Why, of course! If God has turned his face towards men in love and forgiveness, a new day has dawned for them. It is the beginning of new life altogether.

Here, once again, we see how necessary it is to think of the whole of Christ's saving work – the cross as well as the cradle, and the resurrection as well as the cross. It is very significant that in the account of our Lord's resurrection we have the same suggestive thought. In Matthew 28:1 we read, 'In the end of the Sabbath, as it *began to dawn* towards the first day of the week'. This is the final movement of the Incarnation – and this indeed is a new day for the children of men. 'If any man be in Christ, he is a new creature: old things are passed away; behold, all things are become new' (2 Corinthians 5:17). A true understanding of Christmas, and a true experience of Christmas, means the dawning of a new day for our lives.

But how does a new day dawn? Not in a sudden burst of light, but quietly, imperceptibly, first of all with only a few streaks of light in the eastern sky. And so it was with God's new day: he came so silently and unobtrusively that scarce anyone realised he had come.

> How silently, how silently,
>
> the wondrous gift is given!
>
> So God imparts to human hearts
>
> the blessings of His heaven.
>
> No ear may hear His coming;
>
> but in this world of sin,
>
> where meek souls will receive Him, still
>
> the dear Christ enters in.

# The light of new life for all who receive him

We must now consider what the 'new day' brings. It is a new day because of what Christmas and its message brings to human beings.

Zacharias speaks of the 'knowledge of salvation', the 'remission of sins', the 'tender mercy of God', 'light in darkness', and 'the way of peace'. A new day dawns for any man when a knowledge of salvation comes to his heart. A new day dawns for a man when he receives the remission of sins, when he experiences the tender mercy of God, when light shines in his darkness, and when his feet are led into the way of peace.

Before Christ comes to men, it is all darkness for them. Listen to Paul: 'At that time, ye were without Christ, being aliens from the commonwealth of Israel, and strangers from the covenants of promise, having no hope, and without God in the world... having the understanding darkened, being alienated from the life of God, through the ignorance that is in them, because of the blindness of their hearts' (Ephesians 2:12; 4:18). But when the sun of righteousness rises upon them, it is daybreak indeed.

I once came across a suggestive comment on the phrase in Genesis 1, 'the evening and the morning'. Literally, it refers to the fact that the Jewish day was counted from sunset one evening to sunset the next evening. But there may be a further message in the expression. When God starts to work on a man's soul it is in darkness; but when he finishes, it is the morning. The light has come, and a new day has dawned. Sometimes, it is true, the evening seems to last a long while, but God's dealings with us always bring us to the morning. Weeping, as the Psalmist says, may endure for a night, but joy comes in the morning.

'And God said, "Let there be light". And the *evening* and the *morning* were the first day'. Let us remember the story of the fall in Genesis is *our* story. We all fall in Adam, and, thanks be to God, we may all rise in Christ. The darkness came upon all men; the light shines for all men today in the message of the angels. We may ignore it, neglect it, disbelieve it, as Zacharias once did; or we may let it touch our sightless eyes, to bring the light of the knowledge of the glory of God in the face of Jesus Christ.

## Personal visitation

It should be noticed that the central figures in the Christmas story all speak of the visitation of God in personal terms. 'The dayspring from on high hath visited *us*', 'He that is mighty hath done to *me* great things', 'For *mine* eyes have seen Thy salvation'. It is the *personal* relation to the message that makes the new day a reality in the lives of men. Christ came unto his own, John tells us in the prologue to his Gospel – and some received him, responsive to his coming and to his claim. The new day dawned for them; they tasted of the sweet pardon and mercy of God and were turned from darkness into light, from turmoil into peace. All things became new!

This is the real point of Christmas. The question that it asks today is: Do *you* know anything of this divine visitation in your personal life? Has Christmas happened to you yet?

# 4

# The Message of the Angels

*Glory to God in the highest, and on earth
peace, goodwill toward men.*
                                        (Luke 2:14)

It would be a misunderstanding both of the Christmas message
and of our other studies if we thought that Christmas was
something essentially unrelated to our focus as Christians week
by week throughout the year: understanding the Scriptures, and
applying the word of the Lord in them to the present day.

This is surely what we must likewise do with the Christmas
story. If its message has no relevance for our day, we should
be wasting no time coming to church at Christmas, singing
meaningless carols and deceiving ourselves with sentimental
platitudes, while the harsh realities of our tormented world
exercise thinking people outside.

In fact, however, the Christmas message is not different from
that proclaimed throughout the whole Bible, from the prophets
of old. The word of the Lord is ultimately the same in every age;
it is simply that Christmas is its focal point, in the sense that one
can deduce the whole message of the Bible from it.

"

# Restoration

Take our starting point from the words of the angels, 'Glory to God in the highest, and on earth peace, goodwill toward men'. These are perhaps the most familiar words in the entire story. But do we really know what they mean?

They are actually a remarkably full and significant statement of the gospel itself. We can trust the angels for that: they know what the gospel is about! But there are thousands today who do not know – who may be immersed in Christmas activities and even singing Christmas carols, with only the vaguest idea as to why they are doing so.

It is not without significance that so often the world does not speak so much of Christmas as of Xmas. In algebra X is an unknown quantity, and there is surely an unknown quantity about Christmas for many in our time. The Apostle Paul would feel, if he could come back among us, this is a repetition of his experience in Athens, when he saw the city given over to idolatry and, in the midst, an altar with the inscription, 'To the unknown God'. Christ, the chief figure, has been left out of Christmas, and God has been left out of his world.

## God's rightful place restored to the world

This is the point and significance of the angels' song: 'Glory to God in the highest', for it declares God to be back again in his own world, and gives him his rightful place. That is the first, and chief note in the gospel message: not primarily that the needs of men might be met, though the gospel does in fact do this, but that God's holy Name might be honoured and magnified among men, and that he should be first, and have the pre-eminence in all things.

This was the message of the prophets of old; their call was to allow God into the life of the nation's consciousness. Is it not also the word of the Lord for our own time? The real tragedy, in our day as then, is that God has been left out of his world's thinking. This is true on the international and national levels: there is no place for God in the councils of the nations, or in the life of our own nation – and 'where there is no vision, the people cast off restraint' (Proverbs 29:18). It is true also on the personal level: this is the essence, the tragedy of sin, that God is left out of one's life, left out sometimes, indeed, as we pay lip-service to him.

This goes very deep down into the heart of things. For the entrance of sin into the world meant that man chose disobedience instead of obedience, chose to be without God and leave him out of his life. God driven out by sin; yes, but also God withdrawn *from* men, for he is of purer eyes than to behold evil.

It is here that we see the significance of the angel song. It is good tidings of great joy: 'Unto you is born this day a Saviour' – and in this gift of a babe, God comes back into his world again. Likewise, the gospel of Christ gives him his rightful place once more in the hearts and lives of men and women. When this gospel is believed, and the Saviour received, it puts things right – reversing the topsy-turvy order of things that has caused such ruin and havoc in the world and, putting God at the centre, making harmony. It means peace on earth.

Peace is always associated with God having his rightful place in life:

> 'Being justified by faith, we have peace with God' (Romans 5:1)

> 'In everything…let your requests be made known unto God, and the peace of God…' (Philippians 4:6, 7)

> 'O that thou hadst hearkened to my commandments! Then had thy peace been as a river' (Isaiah 48:18)

Give God the glory, put him first – that is the gospel condition for blessing and salvation.

# Revelation

Yet it is significant that when he came, there was 'no room for them in the inn'. This stands as an eloquent symbol of the situation of the world, then and now, and of the need for his coming. Not without cost did he establish his bridgehead of grace again in the world; this is why Jesus died on the cross. It took the cross finally to effect the great reconciliation.

## God's good will towards man revealed to the world

But how is peace on earth to be achieved? The angels said, 'goodwill toward men'. What does this mean? Doubtless Christmas is a season of goodwill among men, and we ought to be friendly and affable at Christmas time, but this is not the primary meaning of the words; it is not goodwill shown by man to man, but goodwill shown by *God* to man.

It is God's will that was declared by the angels of heaven on the plains of Bethlehem. It was God saying, 'For a small moment have I hid My face from thee, but with everlasting kindness will I have mercy on thee' (Isaiah 54:7, 8). The babe of Bethlehem is God's 'olive branch' stretched out to man, to heal the breach that sin has made. It is God's peace overture: 'God was in Christ, reconciling the world unto Himself' (2 Corinthians 5:19).

God's goodwill to man is the gospel offer of salvation, and all the gospel promises are included in this. What the angels meant was God is not willing that any should perish but that all should come to him and live. It was a declaration that 'God is merciful and gracious, slow to anger and plenteous in mercy. He will not always chide, neither will he keep his anger forever. He hath not dealt with us after our sins nor rewarded us according to our iniquities'. It was God saying 'This is the covenant that I will make with them...I will be merciful to their unrighteousness, and their sins and their iniquities will I remember no more' (Psalm 103:9-10). This is the extent and the measure of God's good will toward men, what he is willing to do, and what he offers to men. And the sign and seal of this covenant of good will is a babe in swaddling clothes, lying in a manger.

This is the real happiness of Christmas, and it is the only message on earth capable of bringing true and lasting blessing to men. 'God so loved the world that he gave his only begotten Son, that whosoever believeth in him should not perish but have everlasting life' (John 3:16).

# Response

We must also look at the response of the shepherds to the message of the angels. Is it too much to say that their reaction expresses the divine hope that men should always respond thus to the proclamation of the gospel? They teach us the one right thing to do on hearing the glad tidings of great joy.

## God's grace responded to in the world

They *came*. They did what some have never yet done, they came to Jesus. 'Let us now go even unto Bethlehem, and see this thing which is come to pass' (Luke 2:15). They came and knelt at his infant feet. Why do people not come to Christ? Is it because Bethlehem is the lowly place? We have to stoop to come to him. Is this the problem with many? Is it pride that holds them back?

Second, they came *with haste*. This also reflects the urgency of the gospel message. There is no time to lose. 'Let us *now* go even unto Bethlehem...' (Luke 2:16). Now, not later: this is the gospel summons. 'Today, if you will hear his voice...' (Psalm 95:7-8; Hebrews 3:7). This is something that is hard to understand – why those who know in their mind and heart that the gospel is the hope of mankind, and are intellectually convinced that it is the answer to their personal lives, nevertheless put off the decisive encounter that would lead them into life. One can only conclude that it is a work of satanic deception to hinder them (2 Corinthians 4:4).

Finally, we see from this passage something of the results of the gospel.

## *faith born*

First of all, note the *faith* and *rejoicing* of the shepherds. Faith was born in their hearts before ever they saw the infant Saviour. 'Let us now go even unto Bethlehem and *see* this thing that is come to pass' – not *whether* this thing has come to pass. They believed the word of the angels. Faith comes by hearing (Romans 10:17) – and faith for them was rewarded by sight. Thus they went away rejoicing. It was good news to them; Christmas had happened in their hearts.

## *mission begun*

In the second place, they began to *witness*. They could not keep this news quiet; it was a day of good tidings, and they could not hold their peace. This is how the gospel spreads. First of all we are enlightened; then we must shine. We cannot keep it to ourselves. It must be shared.

This is what God requires of us – to go out and tell a lost and tormented world that he cares, and that Christ is mighty to save. But first it must become good news to *us*.

# 5

# The Virgin Birth of Christ

*Thou shalt call his name JESUS, for He*
*shall save his people from their sins.*

(Matthew 1:21)

Three attitudes are evident in the celebration of Christmas. There is, on the one hand, what may be called the 'secular' attitude – unthinking for the most part, with festivities prominent, and a round of parties, presents, cards, fairy lights and trees, and a squalid commercialisation that encroaches more and more upon our busy autumn days in its determination to make good business of it. On the other hand, there is what seems increasingly evident as a 'wistful' attitude: people listen to the carols and the Christmas story with a wistful, often aching longing that somehow it might cease being merely a story and happen to them.

And there is the 'Christian' attitude, which celebrates with joy not only the birth of Christ, but also our rebirth in him. This is the significance of Christmas for us who are Christians. Christ was

Born to raise the sons of earth,
Born to give them second birth.

Christmas *has* happened to us – our hearts have become the dwelling place of God's Son, and he has been born in us. The Dayspring from on high has visited us, to give light to our darkness and guide our feet into the way of peace.

Our prayer should be that both the 'secular' attitude and the 'wistful' be transformed into the 'Christian'. It is certainly with this that Matthew's wonderful words here in the first chapter of his Gospel are concerned.

# Powerful divine birth

First of all, then, let us think about the manner of his birth. Both Matthew and Luke underline the unusual, indeed the unique, nature of his birth: Luke as it particularly affected Mary, and Matthew as it affected Joseph. Both bring before us the mystery and miracle of the virgin birth of Christ. What is the meaning and significance of this? I want to offer three thoughts in this connection.

## A supernatural Saviour...

The doctrine of the virgin birth bears witness to the essentially supernatural nature of the Christian faith, and tells us that in the divine provision of salvation, man as man is set aside.

> The male, as the specific agent of human action in history, with his responsibility for directing the human species, must now retire into the background as the powerless figure of Joseph... God did not choose man in his pride and defiance, but man in his weakness and humility, not man in his historical role, but man in the weakness of his

nature as represented by the woman, the human creature who can confront God only with the words, 'Behold the handmaid of the Lord, be it unto me according to Thy word.

(Karl Barth)

The doctrine of the virgin birth tells us that the part in us which wants to do – indeed insists on doing – something active for our own salvation is resolutely and firmly set aside by God. Salvation is of God, and of him alone.

## ...under the shadow of sin

The doctrine of the virgin birth also bears witness to how close Christ came to the pollution of sin when he came to be our Saviour. Let me explain what I mean. The carol says 'He came down to earth from heaven', and just how low he came: he lived on earth, not as a king, but as a carpenter; not in a palace, but in a peasant home; he was born not in childbed, but in a shed, and laid in a manger, not with nurses and doctors in attendance, but beasts. Moreover the circumstances of his birth were such as to cast a shadow upon him and his mother all their earthly days. It was natural that Joseph should have reacted as he did, and want to put her away; hence the angel reassured him. But no angel reassured the world, and the misunderstanding must necessarily have remained (as John 9:34 bears witness). Who would have believed Mary, had she told?

He came down – as low as this! This was all part of what was involved in the awesome mystery of being made sin for us, that we might be made the righteousness of God in him. (2 Corinthians 5:21) How near he came to the pollution of sin when he became our Saviour!

## ... creating a new humanity

But there is something else that the doctrine of the virgin birth means to tell us, and it is this: the fact of Christ's birth being totally different from that of *any* other man proclaims that in this birth God was doing a *new* thing. A new humanity was being called into existence by the grace of God, which means a decisive break with the old.

This is the point that Matthew seems to be making when he suggests, in effect, that the story he is now telling is the story of the second Adam. In Genesis 1:2, 'The Spirit of God moved upon the face of the waters', and here, Mary is found to be with child of the Holy Spirit. As Luke also puts it, 'the Holy Spirit came upon her and the power of the Highest overshadowed her'. It was an act of new creation. The old humanity, despite its glory and promise, had come to grief; now the new humanity – signifying a complete break with the old, and a new beginning – is ushered in. This is the significance of Paul's words in 1 Timothy 3:16, '*God* was manifest in the flesh'.

But more still: the nature of that new humanity, that new creation, is Christ himself, living *in* man. God manifest in the flesh, in our flesh, living in us, made flesh *in* us. 'Christ liveth in *me*' cries Paul in Galatians 2:20 – as he says with like exultation in Colossians 1:27, 'Christ in *you*, the hope of glory'. This is the meaning of Christmas, and this is our ground of rejoicing!

# Promised divine name

In the next place we see the fulfilment of prophecy that took place in his birth. Matthew repeatedly tells us that all this happened so that the Scriptures might be fulfilled: 'Behold, a virgin shall be with child, and shall bring forth a son...' (Matthew 1:23).

It is when we stand back from Bethlehem, so to speak, that we see it in its true perspective: in terms of prophecy and fulfilment. It is only thus that we can truly understand the significance of Christmas, for this is the climactic point in all the purposes of God. This *is* the fullness of the time, when what was promised of old actually came to pass – that which was ordained from the foundation of the world, and intimated to the faithful down the ages with increasing insistence, until a breathless expectation heralded the coming of the Saviour of men. And ever and again the preoccupation was with his *name*:

> They 'shall call *his name* Immanuel... God *with* us.' (Isaiah 7:14)
>
> '*his* name shall be called Wonderful...' (Isaiah 9:6)
>
> 'Thou shalt call *his name* JESUS...' (Matthew 1:21)

But similarly – with perspective – we must look still further, for Bethlehem is not the *end* of the story, but the *beginning* of the fulfilment. Consider what Paul says in Philippians 2:5-11: 'He...took upon him the form of a servant and was made in the likeness of men...and became obedient unto death... Wherefore God also hath highly exalted him, and given him a *name* which is *above every name...*'

What does this mean? Jesus is the name whose meaning was fulfilled in his ascension and exaltation – that is to say, when all his work was ended. The name given to Joseph by the angel was a prophecy; at the Ascension it became an evangel! The logical conclusion of Matthew's message in this text is found in passages such as Acts 4:8-12, which records the apostolic preaching of the risen and exalted Lord: 'There is *none other name* under heaven given among men, whereby we must be saved'.

# Personal divine touch

Finally, Matthew tells us that he is called Jesus 'for he shall save his people from their sins'. We should bear in mind that Matthew is writing his gospel record from the standpoint and in the perspective of the resurrection and Pentecost, and what he is saying is: here is the explanation of the amazing, miraculous things that have been happening in the experience of the early Church – transformations of life, new beginnings, accessions of power. It is that men have been *saved* from their *sins*. This is what my gospel is about. In the birth, life, death, resurrection and ascension of Jesus resides the dynamic of God, the power behind all powers, that brings men into new life and hope and peace and joy.

That glorious passage in Philippians 2:5-11 already mentioned describes the 'movement' of grace like some divine 'parabola' with its downward sweep followed by the upward. It is when this touches our lives that we are blessed and saved, by being caught up into it, and being raised to newness of life. C.S. Lewis, in Chapter 14 of his book *Miracles*, has a remarkable passage which illustrates this point graphically:

> In the Christian story God descends to re-ascend. He comes down, down from the heights of absolute being into time and space, down into humanity... down to the very roots and sea-bed of the Nature He has created. But He goes down to come

up again and bring the whole ruined world up with him: One has the picture of a strong man stooping lower and lower to get himself underneath some great complicated burden. He must stoop in order to lift, he must almost disappear under the load before he incredibly straightens his back and marches off with the whole mass swaying on his shoulders. Or one may think of a diver, first reducing himself to nakedness, then glancing in mid-air, then gone with a splash, vanished, rushing down through green and warm water into black and cold water, down through increasing pressure into the death-like region of ooze and slime and old decay; then up again, back to colour and light, his lungs almost bursting, till suddenly he breaks the surface again, holding in his hand the precious thing that he went down to recover. He and it are both coloured now that they have come up into the light: down below, where it lay colourless in the dark, he lost his colour too.'

When this divine 'movement' touches us, as it so often touches lives by the operation of the Holy Spirit in the word of the gospel, Christmas 'happens' to us; Christ is born in us, and we are born again in him into newness of life.

Picture a lonely little boy pressing his nose against the window pane of a great house, watching a magnificent family party in progress inside. It is wonderful to watch from the outside – to see the games and the toys and the Christmas tree, and all the children having their happy time – yet, O the wistfulness and the longing as he watches! But what if the son of the house should see him, and come out – and *invite him in* to share in all the party joys!

That is the message of Christmas!

**6**

# No Room in the Inn

*...there was no room for them in the inn.*

(Luke 2:7)

It is salutary, in the midst of the celebrations of Christmas, to realise that on the first Christmas of all, there was no room for the Son of God when he came into the world.

The Church and the Christian world have hallowed, and rejoiced in, the coming of Christ down the ages; but today the wheel has come round full circle, for once again Christ is left out of Christmas, and once again there is no room for him in the inn. I want to think for a little about this.

## Turning Jesus away

Let us try to reconstruct the scene as it was on the first Christmas Eve long ago. Luke tells us it was a time of census, and every man went to his own native place to be registered. There was clearly a great deal of movement of the population, and accommodation would be at a premium especially in some of the smaller places. When Joseph and Mary came to Bethlehem they were too late, it seems, to get anywhere to stay. They were turned away by the innkeeper. 'Sorry, we are full up' he would have said, 'crowded with census people'. Perhaps it was he, in the kindness of his heart, who suggested the 'stable' (which, in fact, is never mentioned!) as some have conjectured. But he would have seen Mary's condition surely – after all the babe was born a few hours later – and it is straining credulity to picture him as a kindly but harassed innkeeper, when you think of this. He would have his own private rooms; *some* people would have been provided for in such circumstances, however crowded they were! But Joseph and Mary were turned away – with Mary in her condition.

Now, the question I want to ask is: would the innkeeper have taken them in if he had known who it was that was to be born? It would surely have been easy for him, as it is also easy for us, to say, 'If only I had known, I would have done very differently'. Three things can be said about this.

# Ignorant refusal of the Christ

The first thing is this: it is true the innkeeper did not know who it was to be born that morning; there was ignorance involved. There was a hiddenness about the coming of the Saviour into the world. Who would have supposed or suspected that this would be the way that God would come into the world to redeem men? Who indeed would suppose that a helpless baby was the divine answer to the need of the world?

This 'hiddenness' is an integral part of the gospel message; it is of its very essence. And this is particularly true of the Christmas theme. It is, moreover, a hiddenness to which men cannot come save by humble, childlike faith.

> How silently, how silently,
> the wondrous gift is given;
> so God imparts to human hearts
> the blessings of his heaven.
> No ear may hear his coming;
> but in this world of sin,
> where *meek souls* will receive him, still
> the dear Christ enters in.

This is why the world passes off with a shrug the Christmas message, although it likes the trappings and the empty festivities. And this is why the innkeeper failed to see any significance in the little company that came to his door. How should he know, except by faith, that this was the weakness of God that was to prove stronger than men? How should he know, either, that this seemingly ordinary happening, of no conceivable importance to the world, should prove to be the link that binds earth to heaven eternally?

## Willing blindness

But this does not mean that it was simply unfortunate, something that could not be helped – and nothing more. No one can ever say such a thing or take such an attitude where the divine visitation is concerned. For it is not true, and never true, that he *cannot* be perceived or discerned, when God comes to men. The shepherds discerned him, Simeon and Anna, and others, discerned him. Jesus himself said to the people of Jerusalem 'If thou hadst known...the things which belong unto thy peace! But now they are *hid from thine eyes*...because thou knowest not the time of thy visitation' (Luke 19:41-44). Do you see his point? Opportunity had knocked, and they had missed it. And opportunity knocked that day at the inn, and the innkeeper knew not the time of his visitation.

There was an old man who lived near our home when we were boys. One day, after I became a Christian, he told me that for years he had been a church-going man, brought up to be faithful at the house of God – and yet he had never seen the truth of the gospel, or the meaning of salvation, until a time came when God opened his sightless eyes to see Christ. He did not know, he was in ignorance; he had been listening to the message week in, week out, and had never really heard it, never discerned in all the weekly worship in God's house, in its preaching, its meditation, in the reading of the Word, that Christ was confronting him, coming to him, knocking at the door of his life.

There are so many of whom this is true, of whom Christ would say with tears, 'If thou hadst known...the things that belong unto thy peace...thou knowest not the time of thy visitation'. Do you recall the solemn words in the parable, 'I never knew you' which, literally rendered, could read 'I not at any time knew you' – as if the Lord were saying 'I offered so often to get through to you, but you would not let me in to know you'. Ignorance in the face of knowledge; darkness in the presence of light. 'He came unto his own, and his own received him not'. O the regrets one day, when men realise what they have done!

In reading this, perhaps you may begin to feel uneasy at the thought that you might be doing this very thing – an uneasy stirring, as if in sleep, when the waking world is trying to break in. If so, God is saying to you, 'Awake, thou that sleepest, and arise from the dead, and Christ shall give thee light' (Ephesians 5:14).

But this leads us naturally on to more that must be said on this subject.

## Arrogant rejection of the Christ

The innkeeper did not know. And men often do not know that it is Christ who is speaking to them in the word of the gospel. But we still have not answered the question whether he would have taken him in if he *had* known who he was. And the answer is: not necessarily.

Sometimes, it is true, there is no room in the inn because of ignorance of who he is; sometimes there is no room today because of ignorance of the gospel. But it is just as true to say that sometimes there is no room, not because men do not know who it is who knocks at the door, but because they *do*. And knowing this, they still refuse him; indeed, just because they know who he is, they refuse him.

When we turn, for example, from Luke's record of the Nativity to Matthew's, and savour the atmosphere of the latter's opening chapters, we find something very different from the eager responsiveness of the shepherds and Simeon and Anna. We find a Jerusalem troubled at the news of his birth, and Herod not only troubled, but already planning and plotting his destruction. Herod *knew* who he was, and this was his reaction and response. For however dimly – and it was but dimly – he sensed and discerned just what Christ's coming was to mean to his own evil rule. He was not prepared to face the change that this would entail. Therefore he planned to destroy the infant Saviour.

## Unwelcome challenge

Here, then, is another reason for there being no room in the inn. Men know who he is, know the claims he is going to make, know the revolution he is going to effect, if he does come in – and they are not prepared to face this. They are against him. They have no room for him, just because they *do* know who he is.

We have perhaps all known men and women like this. Christ has come to them and knocked – and at first, it may be, they did not know who he was; then they gradually or suddenly perceived who he was – and is – and they have looked him in the eye, knowing what he has come for, and said to him, 'No admittance', 'No room for you'. 'He came unto his own, and his own received him not' (John 1:11).

And with us it is far more serious than with the innkeeper. For we know more about him than ever the innkeeper did. We know the gospel record: he left his home in glory for our sakes; though he was rich, yet for our sakes he became poor; he humbled himself and became obedient unto death, even the death of the cross, for us. That is his appeal to our hearts, as he knocks again this Christmas time, and no one can justifiably plead ignorance as an excuse for not having room for him.

## **Persistent resistance to the Christ**

The fact that there was no room for the holy family in the inn is much more than the evidence of his lowly birth – his humiliation, as theologians put it. It was that, of course, and is some indication of how low he stooped for our sakes. It is also a symbol – of something basic and fundamental; it bears witness to something that is too little considered in the Christmas story – namely the *conflict* that his coming aroused in the world.

This is clearly indicated both in the Christmas narratives themselves, as we see in Luke 2:34-35, 'This child is set for the fall and rising again of many in Israel', and John 1:5,11, in the unfolding conflict between light and darkness, as well as in our Lord's own words, 'I came not to send peace, but a sword' (Matthew 10:34).

## Conflict and crisis

This is how the conflict arises: it is one thing to think theoretically of the coming of the Son of God into the world to be our Saviour, and love and admire the matchless story; but if it is considered as an invasion from beyond – as indeed it is – then implied in this is the thought that those in enemy-occupied territory may have got used to the domination of the dark powers, and settled down under them to live a comparatively comfortable life. And so, when the invasion comes, they are placed in an awkward position. They have to make up their minds whether they are glad or sorry that it has begun – make up their minds, moreover, which side they are to be on.

This is the crisis that Christmas precipitates, and it is this that is reflected in the symbol of the inn where there was no room for the Son of God.

Consider two incidents in the New Testament which illustrate this, where the charm of the Christmas story gives way to the realism of its message, and in which the sense of disturbance and crisis is seen to be very decisive indeed. In the story of the maniac of Gadara (Mark 5:1ff) we read that when the tormented man was healed, the Gadarenes prayed Jesus to *depart* from their coasts. In the story of the conversion of the Philippian jailer (Acts 16:25ff) we are told that the magistrates of the city came and implored the apostles to *depart* out of the city. Each story shows two things: (a) the meaning and import of Christmas for a crying human need; and (b) the rejection of the Christmas message by those who found it much too disturbing and dismaying when they discovered what it was all about. When they realised that this – this incommensurable reality that had happened in their midst – was what Christmas really meant, they had no room for the Son of God, and asked him to go away.

## Contemporary confrontation

Christmas is very contemporary. It confronts us. The heart of the gospel is imbedded in it, and just as in the beginning it meant a knock on a door in Bethlehem, so now it means the same: 'Behold, I stand at the door and knock: if any man hear my voice, and open the door, I will come in' (Revelation 3:20). It is the Dayspring from on high come to visit us.

But with a visitor at the door, you are committed to some kind of response: Either you do not answer the door; or you go to the door and when you see who it is you turn him away; or you open the door and invite him in.

In the last analysis there are not many things one can do with a visitor at the door. These are the only options. And already we will have made one of them ours.

7

# The Incarnation of the Word

*And the Word was made flesh, and dwelt
among us, and we beheld his glory, the
glory as of the only begotten of the
Father, full of grace and truth.*

(John 1:14)

Unlike Matthew and Luke, the Apostle John does not narrate the matchless story of Bethlehem, but he does grapple with its meaning and significance, and is conscious supremely of the mystery that makes it a gospel.

It is the sublime depth of the mystery of the Incarnation that forces itself upon us as we read John's words here. There is something awesome about the implications of what he says; one gets the impression of a man whose mind probes deeply into vast and unexplored treasures, and becomes overwhelmed by what he finds there. Let us look, then, at what John has to tell us.

# The eternal Word made flesh

While Matthew and Luke tell us of the birth of the babe, John tells us who he is. It is the Word, the eternal One by whom the worlds were made, that has become flesh in the baby of Bethlehem, as we learn from verses 1-3 and 14 of John's Prologue, which belong in thought together: 'In the beginning was the Word...and the Word was God...and the Word was made flesh'.

What John is speaking of is the movement of, and from, eternity for our sakes, the movement from eternity into history! If we can conceive of history as a story, and then of the possibility of the author of the story somehow breaking into it and becoming part of it, we will, even then, only have a dim perception of the immensity and unthinkable-ness of the mystery of the Incarnation. It is this that makes the gospel so decisive and final for men's lives. Nothing could ever be the same again for them, when once this touches them. How could it be? I do not mean that through the gospel everybody will be set to rights – John makes it clear that this is not so: 'He came unto his own, and his own received him not'. But it does mean that Christ has a decisive effect on men, one way or the other, for weal or woe. The *status quo* is no longer possible in the story when the author comes on to the scene himself.

But why should he have come as a baby, in weakness, and incognito? Why not reveal himself as he is, in power, to put the world to rights?

## Recreator incognito

One day he will do just this; but then it will be too late to believe on him. Men must examine his credentials now – what he does in disguise, his mighty words and works, and his death on the cross – and make up their minds about him as their Saviour. This Saviour of whom I speak, says John, is the Eternal Word, made flesh for our sakes. He who in the beginning made all worlds has come down as Man, to remake fallen man and give him new life.

> Born to raise the sons of earth,
>
> Born to give them second birth.

The work of creation in the beginning is simply the reflections of an infinitely greater work of *recreation* in the gospel. It is this that explains the 'signs', the acts of grace that John records in his gospel; they illustrate the trinity of life, light and power unfolded in his Prologue now at work in the lives of men, showing Isaiah's words to be true: 'My word... shall not return unto me void, but it shall accomplish that which I please, and it shall prosper in the thing whereto I sent it' (Isaiah 55:11).

We should note the parallelism between the opening verses of John's Prologue and verse 14: It is he who *is God* who has become *flesh*, it is he who was *with God* who has tabernacled among us; it is he who was *in the beginning* who became flesh in history. This is the amazing mystery that fills John's heart – and surely ours also! – with wonder and awe. He could never get over this astounding, incredible fact that God, the great Creator of the universe, should come down and be made *man*. Like the

Psalmist of old, he would say, 'Such knowledge is too wonderful for me; it is high, I cannot attain unto it' (Psalm 139:6).

> Let earth and heaven conspire,
> angels and men agree,
> to praise something divine
> the incarnate deity;
> Our God contracted to a span,
> incomprehensibly made man.

# The mystery of the Incarnate God

What do we mean when we say that the Word was made, or became, flesh? What did John mean to convey by these words?

Whatever may be said about this, it must be emphasised that John does not, and cannot, mean that he ceased to be what he was before, and became something else. In this connection, there are two points that need to be made.

## Ceaselessly God

In the first place, the Eternal Son did not cease to be God, although he became man. To say he came in disguise, incognito, conveys something of the mystery, although in another sense this is just as misleading, as we shall see in a moment. But, so far as it goes, what we may say is that beneath and behind the disguise there is the Person of God the Son. Thus in 1 John 4:2, and 2 John 7, the words 'come in the flesh' mean that it is he, the Second Person of the Trinity, that is come in human form – he, *not* another. Paul underlines the same thing in 1 Timothy 3:16; it is *God* who was 'manifest in the flesh'.

It is in this light that we must consider what Paul says in Philippians 2:5ff. The words 'he made himself nothing' [ESV] ('he emptied himself', [RSV]) cannot be construed to mean that he became something *less* than he originally was. It is for this reason that the theology of the Church has never been quite happy with phrases such as we have in Wesley's hymns, 'emptied himself of all but love' or 'mild he lays his glory by' – if these statements are construed to suggest that Christ the Son divested himself of his deity in any way. There was never a moment, not even in the cradle in the manger, when he ceased to be God. Wesley's other phrase in the same hymn, 'veiled in flesh the *Godhead* see' is much safer ground to take.

Christ was never less than God. His 'self-emptying' was the laying aside of the mode of divine existence which he enjoyed with the Father, but it was not a laying aside of what he was, and is.

## Permanently man

In the second place, the idea of a disguise is misleading in that, for us, a disguise is something we dispense with when it is no longer needed. But Jesus Christ does not lay aside his human 'disguise': he has become Man forever. 'Manhood taken by the Son' was not a temporary expedient, but something done once for all and forever. In this is the permanent hallowing and sanctifying of humanity.

On the other hand, the word 'flesh' must be taken with equal seriousness. God the Son really became man. The humanity of Christ was, and is, real and complete. He was, and is, fully and permanently man. This is mystery indeed, but the mystery must be accepted. Jesus is divine and Jesus is human, both God and man. He has two natures, the divine and the human, united in one Person, the God-Man. The Word is not made flesh by changing one nature into another, or by laying aside one nature and taking up another. The Incarnation is the mystery of God *manifest* in the flesh.

## The divine, substitute Man

Now let us take another step in our thinking. A further implication of the Incarnation which is of profound importance is this: The Word was made flesh, that is to say, he became man. Not *a* man, merely – although, of course, Christ was that – but *Man*.

Christ became man in the sense that he displaces men from the centre of the divine stage, displaces the world of men, and assumes their part in the drama that is being enacted. Man, as such, is set aside, and becomes a spectator, an onlooker, while the 'role' of man is taken by Jesus.

This is the doctrine of substitution, and is implicit in the whole conception of the Incarnation; and when it is looked at in this way it comes home with marvellous force and power. For it means that Jesus, the Jesus of history, is now the 'mankind' that God has dealings with. He 'enters the lists', so to speak, on our behalf, as our Champion and Representative, standing in as our Substitute to fulfil all righteousness for us – both from a negative and from a positive point of view: negatively, in that he assumes all our liabilities as his own, and positively, in that he gives to God all that a holy God could require of us.

> O generous love! that He who smote
> in Man, for man, the foe,
> the double agony in man
> for man should undergo.

In man – for man – as man! Such is the 'movement of eternity' for our sakes. God manifest in the flesh – well might we bow in awe and worship before him!

## The reconciling God-Man

What we have already said leads us on inevitably to the fact of the Atonement. For Christ became man in order to be our Saviour from sin. It was a Saviour who was born in Bethlehem; one who was to save people from their sins. And so the 'Word made flesh' is fulfilled in the Word made *sin*.

It is here that we see that what we said earlier about Christ the second Person of the Trinity remaining God in his innate state is no mere theological quibble, but lies at the very heart of the message of grace. Christ required to be, and remain, God, in the mystery of his Person, to make atonement for sin and be a Saviour. A God divested of his deity, a Jesus who emptied himself of his deity, could not save. For sin, being sin against an infinite and eternal God, partakes of that infinity and eternity, and therefore no-one merely human – and therefore finite – could deal with the problem of human guilt. No-one less than an *infinite* and *eternal* God could make atonement.

At the same time, however, atonement to be real must necessarily be made by *man*, and from man's side, since it is man who has sinned. Here, then, is the dilemma: what needed to be done *had* to be done by man, but was so big, so infinite, that *no* man could possibly do it; only a God could assume such a task. And in Christ, the God-Man, both the divine and the human necessities of the situation are met. It is not the Godhead *per se*, but the God-Manhood of Christ the Mediator, that achieves atonement and reconciliation. This is the 'mystery of godliness' (1 Timothy 3:16), and great indeed it is, passing all knowledge.

## God's true glory beheld on earth

In this connection, and in one final word we must look at John's statement 'we beheld his glory'. What does this mean?

Does he refer to the miracle of Bethlehem? Or, as some think, to the story of the Transfiguration? Or are we to take his meaning, with others, as referring to the outshining of his Person throughout the whole of his ministry? Doubtless all these suggestions have some force and worth in them, but if what we have just been saying is true, then it must be clear that the supreme outshining of that glory was *in the cross*. This is borne out by our Lord's own words in John 12:23ff: 'The hour is come, that the Son of man should be *glorified...* Except a corn of wheat fall into the ground and die, it abideth alone ... And I, if I be lifted up from the earth, will draw all men unto me'.

For John, the cradle and the cross belong together. *Here*, for him, is the fountain of grace and truth, flowing for the children of men; *here* we learn the depth of the meaning of 'Immanuel, God with us'.

> Like Mary, let us ponder in our mind
>
> God's wondrous love in saving lost mankind;

trace we the Babe, who has retrieved our lost,

from his poor manger to his bitter Cross;

treading his steps, assisted by his grace,

till man's first heavenly state again takes place.

# 8

# To Enrich the Humble Poor

*The angel Gabriel was sent from God...*
*to a virgin espoused to a man whose name*
*was Joseph, of the house of David: and the*
*virgin's name was Mary.*

(Luke 1:26,27)

I once listened to a documentary programme about the Church of England – and a rather gloomy programme it was! But it did contain one ray of light, in the words of a vicar in a big housing estate who went forth regularly with a loudspeaker, proclaiming the gospel message: and saying that the gospel was for ordinary people, that it came to ordinary people, and that it was ordinary people who first received it.

This, it might be thought, is a statement of the obvious: but it is often the obvious that gets right home to our hearts. And that thought certainly stuck in mine, for it cannot be denied that the personalia in the Christmas message were all humble, ordinary folk – not middle class, not academics, not professional men and women, but ordinary, humble, peasant folk. Think of Mary, and Joseph the carpenter; Simeon and Anna; Zacharias and Elizabeth; the shepherds in the field.

It was *to* ordinary folk, and *for* ordinary folk, that Jesus came.

## Jesus the populist

The movement that took place around Jesus was a popular movement: it is said of him that 'the common people heard him gladly' (Mark 12:37). After his death and resurrection, when the apostles preached his Name, the great majority of the converts were ordinary folk, indeed from the slave classes. So striking was this that Paul could say to the Corinthians, 'that not many wise men after the flesh, not many mighty, not many noble are called' (I Corinthians 1:26). What, then, does this say to us?

We need to be careful in our thinking here, otherwise we could get into a real tangle of confusion and misunderstanding. What we are faced with today is the charge that the Church's message precisely does *not* command the attention and allegiance of ordinary working people; that the Church has almost completely lost the working classes, and that it is, by and large, a middle-class institution.

There are some inferences we can draw from this that are legitimate, as well as some that are illegitimate and unwarranted.

# Institutional loss of the gospel

For example, as to the legitimate inferences, we have to say this: it may well be that the real message of the gospel has become obscured and crusted over in the Church, and by the Church, in its repeatedly having become a mere institution.

It is certainly true that when the real message of the gospel has been recovered, in history, the common people once again *have* heard gladly, as, for example, at the time of the Reformation, or the Great Awakenings. I wonder, in view of this, whether part at least of the explanation of why so many ordinary folk are drawn to *Christmas* worship – beyond and behind the sentiment and romance of Christmas – is that something of the original appeal of the gospel is there attracting them, drawing them, ringing a bell for them? And could we not crystallise this in one simple word: the Christmas message of old was a message of good news. It was this that made its appeal; and it is this that makes the appeal today, and this that, alas, is otherwise so often lost and obscured: 'Good tidings of great joy'.

But, having said this, we must be careful not to make wrong inferences. It is an easy mistake, but a profound one, to assume that since the gospel, and its Christmas message, made its appeal to the common people, that gospel is necessarily simple in the sense that it is undemanding intellectually, and that anything that calls for serious thought is necessarily an encrusting over of the simple message with abstruse dogma and theology.

This is a mistake that has often been made in the past, and in the present too; and it has often been made a pretext for debunking a theological and doctrinal approach to the message of the gospel. 'Let's have the simple message of Jesus' many have said, 'not the theological agglomerations of Paul'. But see the implication of this wrong attitude, this mistake!

# Unwarranted dumbing down of the gospel

This is to make the assumption that ordinary folk are not very intelligent, and that they cannot think!

Is this, then, what we really believe? What a travesty of the truth, and what an unwarranted indictment of ordinary folk! One has only to think of the history of Scottish piety from the Reformation onwards to realise how utterly mistaken this is. It is common knowledge that almost every humble home in Scotland fed on, and understood, and gloried in, the truths of the *Shorter Catechism*, and that books like Thomas Boston's *Fourfold State of Man* were staple spiritual diet for ordinary, devout folk, and understood by them, and fed upon!

Just think, too, how many men of God have been raised in our past history, in the humble homes of the land, how many men of intellect and academic brilliance who have come to the forefront as leaders of the nation!

Look at the theological perception of *these* ordinary people in the Christmas story itself, as witnessed by their own poetic compositions – Mary and the *Magnificat*, Zacharias and the *Benedictus*, Simeon and the *Nunc Dimittis*. These songs are full of theology: deep, profound thinking about God and grace and salvation.

Look at the carols we sing – they too are theologically saturated! The *First Nowell* is a traditional folk carol narrating simply the Christmas story; yet it declares a weighty message, ending as it does in a wonderfully discerning expression of the paradox of simplicity and profundity, about the One

> That hath made heaven and earth of
> nought, and with his blood mankind
> hath bought.

One thinks similarly of the lovely hymn that confesses 'I am not skilled to understand, what God hath willed, what God hath planned'; here is the plea of inability to grasp the deep things – and yet the hymn is deeply theological and perceptive, and speaks of the profoundest realities of Christian experience.

## Appetite for mind-enlarging truth

All of this tells us something: the gospel is something which creates in men an appetite for its truth, and does something to ordinary folk, enlarging their minds and their understanding, and indeed their whole personality.

It is sometimes claimed today that the Church is largely a middle-class group of people. One is never quite sure what is meant by the phrase – whether it is a political conception, or an economic one, or a social one. But I think there is a good deal of confusion in the statement itself. The common people still hear the gospel gladly – the need is the same, whatever social station we belong to – and in this regard it is simply *not* true to say that the Church's appeal is to the middle classes.

But what does happen when men hear the gospel is this: they do not 'become' middle class, from being ordinary working folk.

But if their response to the gospel is real, their whole life-style will change; their pattern of living will be transformed. They do not, as C.S. Lewis says somewhere, get their qualities from a class: they belong to that class because they have those qualities. For in a society like ours no stock which has diligence, forethought or talent, and is prepared to practise self-denial, is likely to remain proletarian for more than a generation. They in fact become the bearers of what little moral, intellectual or economic vitality remains in our society today.

The undiscerning, the bigoted, the prejudiced will dub them 'middle class'. What has happened may be that they have visibly changed – from bingo, and the pub, and the pools, to values that are real and worthwhile. But what has really happened to them is not a change in social class, but a change in status. They have become *new*, with a wholly new life-style.

They are still ordinary people, but for them, through the gospel of Christ, old things have passed away, and all things are become new. This is the enrichment that the message of Christmas brings; and it is the only enrichment that matters.

# 9

# The Meaning of Christmas

*Where is he that is born king of the Jews?*
*For we have seen his star in the east, and*
*are come to worship him.*

*(Matthew 2:2)*

The wise men from the east said, 'Where is he that is born king...?' They spoke more truly than they could have known.

They could hardly have realised just what their words must have done to Herod and those who heard them in Jerusalem. For if they were unaware, Herod and the inhabitants of Jerusalem would not have been unaware, that their question echoed words spoken in ancient time by the prophet Isaiah, who said, in words sublime and glorious, 'Unto us a child is born, unto us a son is given.... and the government shall be upon his shoulder' (Isaiah 9:6).

It was a king who was promised, and it was a king who came!

# Jesus – infant, yet the true King of the world

The kingship of Christ! It is impressive to see how substantially this is taken up in the teaching of the New Testament as a whole, by the Gospel writers and the apostles alike. It becomes clear, on an unprejudiced reading of the Scriptures, that it is not open to us to think of Jesus in anything but kingly terms. True, he was born in the humblest of circumstances; but shepherds and wise men alike did obeisance before him, acknowledging his royalty. True, in his lifetime he had nowhere to lay his head; yet nature and the elements, sickness and disease, devils and death all alike owned his kingship and acknowledged his rule.

When the apostles preached him, they preached the kingship of Christ: 'another king, one Jesus' (Acts 17:7). When they wrote of him in the epistles, they referred to him as the One to whom every knee should bow, and every tongue confess that He is Lord.

## God's answer – a baby

Let us leave that thought for the moment, and pursue another. In an earlier chapter we thought on Matthew's words 'Immanuel, God with us', and the gloriously assuring thought which is expressed in many of the best-loved carols:

> This Babe, we now declare to you,
>
> is Jesus Christ the Lord.

But do you see the far-reaching implications of this kind of statement? What is really being said is this: over against the vastness of the tragedy of humanity, with all its sin, with its terrifying enigmas and mysteries, its intractable problems and agonies, God sets as his answer – a baby! There seems a sheer incongruity to it! On the one hand, the bleakness of the human situation, and on the other – a helpless infant!

In answer to this seeming incongruity the Bible tells us that the weakness of God is stronger than men, and the foolishness of God is wiser than men. God has chosen the weak things of the world to confound the mighty, and the foolish things of the world to confound the wise. Things which are despised God has chosen to bring to naught the things that are (1 Corinthians 1:27-9).

This is true, so true. But there is another way of resolving this incongruity. We have already seen how the Gospel writers and the apostles direct our attention constantly back to the Old Testament Scriptures, and to the beginnings of the story of man in Genesis 3. This is where we too must begin.

## Man's rule and realm ruined by sin

Has it ever occurred to us to ask what God originally intended in creation, if sin had not entered to mar it?

Creation was to be the expression of his glory and majesty and sovereignty. It was to magnify and exalt him in a universe which in all its parts was entirely subservient to him – the whole created order, not merely the earth. The vastness of this conception is staggering; it is hinted at here and there in Scripture – the whole system of government in the universe, with authority delegated to angelic beings, powers, authorities – some set over nations, some over groups, some with even larger authority. In all this wonderful creation, man was destined and appointed for rule and authority, as over-lord of creation.

But alas, man came under attack. For, although we are not told explicitly in the Bible, it seems that before time was, a revolt took place in the world of spirits; Lucifer, son of the morning, rebelled, becoming Satan, the Adversary, and began independent existence, founding a kingdom of darkness in opposition to God's kingdom of light. This, or something of this nature, must be understood before we can come to the story of man's fall. For sin entered the world from the outside, that is, from Satan's kingdom. And Satan attacked man because man was God's good creation; Satan determined to ruin it, and him, to spite God, to attack him.

## War against God

This shows something of the truly terrifying nature of sin in man – it was the coming into humanity of Satan's war against God, the assault of evil on all that is good. The attack was made, and man fell; Satan's purpose, it seems, succeeded. So, instead of being, as originally destined, the great and splendid and glorious overlord of God's creation, man became the tool and dupe and slave of the devil, held captive by him to do his evil will.

Man was seduced from obedience to his rightful King, the true and living God. The revolt was complete – the world, and man, were set in rebellion against God. It is not too much to say that humanity, and the world, became enemy-occupied territory, the denial, the negation of God's good creation and his blessed purposes.

# The abolition of man

It is this evil reign of sin that is responsible for all the woe in the world – from the beginning until now. Every eruption of sin – from Cain's murderous hatred of his brother to the terrors of modern warfare – is explained by the presence of the dark power behind it all. It is all part of the dark and sinister drive towards the abolition of man, and his destruction out of God's purposes for him.

This is the background against which we need to understand Christmas, and the statement that God's answer to the tragedy and horror of the world of sin was – a baby. For what the Bible wants us to see, right from its first book, Genesis, is this: at the dawn of history, as soon as the darkness fell upon the world, God gave the promise that the seed of the woman would bruise the head of the Serpent. God was promising that he would begin again; that there would be another man; that his original purposes would come to pass for man; that man *would* come into his own as the overlord of creation; that man would achieve and realise his true destiny.

## Man's rule and realm redeemed by the Saviour

Think of the original promise in Genesis 3:15, spoken into the darkness, as a word of hope for man in his sin, that out of man, for man, there would come a new start, a new creation. 'The seed of the woman....'.

Then, centuries later in Isaiah 9:6, came the promise 'Unto us a child is born, unto us a son is given: and the government shall be upon his shoulder'.

And then, at last, this: 'Unto you is born this day in the city of David a Saviour, which is Christ the Lord…ye shall find the babe wrapped in swaddling clothes, lying in a manger'.

## New humanity through the new man

A babe – the weakness of God! Yes, but see also that this at last is God's new man, God's *new* humanity, in whom his destined purposes are to be fulfilled and realised. Christmas is the planting of a new humanity in the world.

If this be so, we can hardly speak of the incongruity of the situation – not if this babe is to be the re-institution of man, the re-investiture of man as overlord of creation! This is what Christmas is. With this as the key, so much begins to gleam with light.

This is what explains the repeat of the pattern that obtained at the beginning, namely the attack of Satan on God's Chosen One. It explains the attempt by Herod to kill the young Child, and his miraculous preservation by the angels of God. It explains the story of the temptation in the wilderness, when the temptation followed the exact pattern of that in the Garden of Eden – to eat unlawfully, to presume upon God, to grasp unlimited power – but with this difference: that whereas the first man fell and was beguiled out of his true destiny by Satan, *this* man stood, and refused to yield. It is this that invests his person and character with infinite power an incalculable potential, and makes him a sufficient answer to the gigantic agonies and needs of the world. For this is something unique: a man who never sinned, the only man who never sinned, and who therefore did not need to die.

Yet this man went into death for our sakes, to unmake the tragedy and horror of death and sin and sorrow and woe, and to take over fallen man's place and role in creation.

This is what the writer to the Hebrews underlines in Hebrews 2:5ff, when he quotes from Psalm 8: 'What is man that Thou art mindful of him...made... a little lower than the angels' – that is, relegated because of his sin in a position lower than the angels, a position not originally his, but something he became because of sin – but yet, through grace, to be crowned with glory and honour, restored, re-instituted to his former position and destiny. But – the Apostle goes on – 'as yet we do not see everything in subjection to him (i.e. to man)'. But what we *do* see is Jesus!

Do you see the implications of the apostle's argument here? On the one hand is man, relegated for a while lower than the angels – and just *how* low we see in our world of sorrow, agony and woe, sin and shame. And on the other hand, is another man, Jesus; and – note well – the 'repeat' here, for of him also it is said that *he* was 'for a little while made lower than the angels, crowned with glory and honour for the suffering of death...'

Paul's tremendous words in Philippians 2:5ff echo this same truth, as he speaks of Christ 'who, being in the form of God... humbled himself, and took upon him the form of a servant, and was made in the likeness of men, and...became obedient unto death...wherefore God also hath highly exalted him, and given him a name which is above every name...'.

## New creation through the new man

All this gives substance to the apostle's words in 1 Timothy 3:16: 'Great is the mystery of godliness'. Great indeed – for it is the power, the incalculable power and potential of the *New Man*!

What price the sense of incongruity now? Little wonder that his coming as a babe threw all Jerusalem into a turmoil! Here is God's Proper Man. Well might the prophet say, 'his name shall be called Wonderful, Counsellor, the Mighty God, the Everlasting Father, the Prince of Peace'.

Creation coming back into its own, and coming to fruition and fulfilment through a man – *The Man* – Christ Jesus, conceived by the Holy Ghost, born of the virgin Mary, of the Father's love begotten.

Such is the significance of the babe of Bethlehem; such is the meaning of Christmas.

Our church is part of the worldwide family united by the cross of Jesus. Students, young workers, families and older saints, from many nationalities and all walks of life – we are all one in Christ Jesus.

Our vision, which drives everything we do, is to see the risen Lord Jesus crowded by people from our city and every nation, ransomed by his blood and raised by his Spirit through the gospel, reigning for eternity with him to the glory of God the Father.

So we worship together to make and grow mature disciples of Jesus Christ in ever greater numbers who with us will glorify God and enjoy him forever.

We are a presbyterian church and are committed and accountable to a wider family of congregations in Scotland called the Didasko Presbytery.

If you are visiting Glasgow, do be sure to visit us on a Sunday.

For more information, visit our website - tron.church

# TRON BOOKS

Launched in 2024, Tron Books seeks to produce and distribute excellent Christian books that both equip and encourage church leaders and members. Our hope is to publish a range of biblically-faithful, stimulating and timeless publications that will help those in the pulpit or pew to prosper in their Christian walk and service.

To find out more, visit our website - tron.church/publish